change
HOW YOU
think

&

BE
happier
now

KATE JAMES

Published by Affirm Press in 2017

28 Thistlethwaite Street, South Melbourne, VIC 3205
www.affirmpress.com.au

National Library of Australia Cataloguing-in-Publication entry
available for this title at www.nla.gov.au.

Title: Change How You Think & Be Happier Now /
Kate James, author.

ISBN: 9781925475425 (hardback)

Design by Karen Wallis

Printed in China through 1010 Printing

change
HOW YOU
think

&

BE
happier
now

KATE JAMES

About
Kate James

Kate James is a coach, meditation teacher, speaker and writer.

Through her business, Total Balance, she helps clients understand how to make mindfulness part of their everyday lives.

You'll find more of Kate's work at totalbalance.com.au.

For Anna

Praise for Kate James
and Total Balance

'I absolutely adore Kate. She is a highly skilled, generous and enormously gifted business coach, especially for those who don't traditionally consider themselves "business people".'

Clare Bowditch, Big Hearted Business

'Kate has assembled a wonderful collection of invaluable insights, practical tools and life-enhancing advice in *Believe in Yourself & Do What You Love* to help us understand ourselves better and to find greater meaning in what we do. I only wish I'd discovered this book thirty years ago!'

David Michie, author of Buddhism for Busy People *and* Hurry Up and Meditate

'*Be Mindful & Simplify Your Life* is a beautiful and very practical book. It will open your heart and your life in unexpected ways.'

Jono Fisher, founder of the Wake Up Project

'In *Believe in Yourself & Do What You Love*, Kate has beautifully captured, in her words and her design, the key elements that lead to success and happiness in life. As many of us know, "common sense" is not very common, but Kate reminds us of what we need to be reminded of if we want to live our best possible lives.'

Dr Timothy Sharp, The Happiness Institute

'Kate James' book *Be Mindful & Simplify Your Life* is jam-packed with practical tools for bringing mindfulness into our busy modern lives. She beautifully weaves science with spirituality and practice to present a compact handbook for mindful living.'

Liv Downing, co-founder of Happy Melon Studios

Contents

Contents

Introduction

The work that I've done with mindfulness over the past fifteen years has changed the way I think about happiness. My aim these days is not to blindly pursue a 'happy' life, but rather to learn about how I can be more at peace on a daily basis, *regardless of what I'm experiencing*.

This may not be the way we'd usually define happiness. We're more inclined to think of a happy life as one where we seek out pleasant experiences and avoid difficult or painful feelings.

It's likely that life will be a rollercoaster ride at times. The real challenge is to stay in touch with the experience of *feeling alive*, no matter the content of that experience. On the days that life is painful, we make room to feel pain. On the days that life scares us, we allow ourselves to feel afraid. On the days that life is joyful, we embrace joy – and we do all of this without holding on too tightly to the good or railing against what's difficult.

When we make contact with the present moment and quieten our concerns about the future and past, we discover that *this is where peace exists*.

Genuine happiness is less about achieving outward measures of success and more about accepting who we are; making the most of our current circumstances; cultivating and embracing loving relationships; giving to others; discovering aspirations and dreams that are meaningful to us; and feeling hopeful and positive about the future.

Within this book you'll find tips about how to achieve much of this – not necessarily in the order noted above, and not every aspect is covered in detail. Consider this a first step on your way to thinking differently about happiness. You may also want to explore the resources listed at the end of the book for ongoing inspiration.

Some of the suggestions may seem contradictory, and in many ways they are. This is one of the confounding factors when we examine what it means to be happy. For example, you'll see that I recommend being more optimistic but I also recommend balancing over-optimism. When you're confronted with a suggestion that seems contradictory, simply choose the direction that feels most natural and most helpful to you.

We need to be mindful about not getting fixed on a rigid or inflexible definition of happiness, and when we do catch a glimpse of it, we need to remind ourselves that it's not something to cling to, but a gift to hold lightly and treasure while it lasts.

Kati

It's a paradox

If you live in the Western world and you're not experiencing poverty, domestic violence, abuse of any kind or any other threat to your safety, you're in a small percentage of the world's most privileged people. Unfortunately, that doesn't mean you're happy.

Those of us who live in the 'developed world' often have high expectations of life, and in some ways these expectations put us under a lot of pressure to be happy. But happiness is not a commodity that we can buy or gain through external means: it's complex and confounding.

1. Often the more we strive to be happy, the harder it feels to achieve.

2. A genuinely contented life is one where we allow for difficult feelings as well as joyous ones.

3. There's plenty of happiness to share around, which means we don't need to compare ourselves to others or compete for it.

4. Happiness is often more readily achieved when we're not solely focused on ourselves. Sometimes it's about putting our own needs first, but it is equally about giving to others.

5. It can involve pushing ourselves as much as seeking comfort.

6. Some of what we call 'happiness' is within our control, and some of it isn't. The key is knowing (and accepting) the difference.

7. How happy we are can change from one minute to the next. It's a constant balancing act.

8. Nobody else is responsible for our happiness – it's something we need to discover for ourselves – but our relationships do play a significant part in how happy we are.

9. We might assume being happier requires significant change, but sometimes the smallest things make the biggest difference.

10. Once we achieve a relative state of contentment, we can be pretty sure things won't stay the same for long. Equally, when we're going through a rough patch we need to remind ourselves that even the most difficult experiences don't last forever.

If you're suffering from mental illness

When you're depressed, it's anything but helpful to be told to 'change how you think'.

Clinical depression is an illness, just as asthma and diabetes are illnesses. In the same way that you can't treat these physical ailments without the support of professionals, depression is difficult to tackle alone. The same can be said for anxiety, PTSD and other mental illnesses.

THE TIPS INCLUDED IN THIS LITTLE GUIDE ARE DESIGNED TO HELP YOU THROUGH THE UPS AND DOWNS OF EVERYDAY LIFE, BUT THEY MAY NOT BE THE PLACE TO BEGIN WHEN YOU'RE IN A SERIOUS SLUMP.

Having said that, the approach in this book is a balanced one. It's not *just* about being more positive. Happiness isn't a state any of us will be in all of the time. And nor do we need to be. One of the keys to happiness is accepting that difficult feelings are a natural part of life.

People suffering from mental illness often experience guilt about feeling the way they do, as though they should be more grateful for the things that are good in their lives or be able to snap out of it. This kind of thinking isn't helpful.

Not everyone has the capacity to change how they think right now. If that's where you find yourself, it might be worth putting aside this book and giving yourself permission to make your way through the difficult patch in your own time. Come back to it later or, if it's not what you think you need, gift it to someone else. Most importantly, continue to reach out for support. It's often a challenging process finding the right person to help you, but don't give up. There's someone out there who will understand your struggles and *they will be able to help*.

See the resources list at the end of this book for suggestions about where to start.

The difference between happiness & pleasure

Most of us pursue happiness by seeking out activities, experiences and possessions that provide us with immediate pleasure. But pleasure is not the same thing as genuine, lasting happiness.

As Positive Psychology researcher Martin Seligman describes in his book *Authentic Happiness*, genuine happiness isn't short-lived in the way that pleasure is. We're more likely to achieve it when we learn how to feel engaged in our lives and when we discover our own version of a meaningful life.

Seligman introduces three major sets of experiences that he calls 'The Pleasant Life', 'The Good Life' and 'The Meaningful Life'.

Pleasure (or 'The Pleasant Life') is what we experience when we fall in love, spend time partying with friends, achieve a promotion or land our dream job. It's the sensation we might feel when we buy new clothes, get a new car or win the lottery. But in all these situations the feeling is fleeting; we adapt incredibly quickly to new circumstances and then become focused on finding the next thing that will give us a high (more about this in chapter 5).

According to Seligman, an engaged life (or what he calls 'The Good Life') occurs when we understand and deploy our natural strengths every day, and 'The Meaningful Life' comes about when we make a contribution to something bigger than ourselves.

Lasting happiness can be achieved when we find a balance between all three areas, but ultimately Seligman believes that our focus should be less on hedonistic pleasure-seeking, and more on discovering engagement and meaning.

Challenge your baseline

It's been estimated that around half of our baseline happiness is genetically inherited and only a tiny amount (around 10 per cent) is related to our circumstances. This suggests that a large portion of our capacity for happiness may actually be under our direct control.

One of the keys to increasing your baseline is having a sense of control over where you are going in life – something that's not super easy to achieve but is at least worth fighting for.

TAKE RESPONSIBILITY

It's impossible to feel a sense of control when you put your destiny in the hands of others. Instead of waiting for your life circumstances to change, or for opportunities to come from others, think about how you can move your life in a positive direction.

BUILD YOUR CAPACITY FOR COURAGE

Courage comes from behaving courageously. Think of building courage in the same way you think of building strength at the gym. You start by lifting the smallest weights before building up to the big ones. Find small action steps to carry out that expose you to the things that scare you before tackling the things that are genuinely confronting.

FIND YOUR PURPOSE IN LIFE

A purposeful life is one where you make a contribution to society in a way that is meaningful and unique to you. Think about how you can bring your individual gifts to life every day in a way that makes a difference to other people (more about how to do this in chapter 31).

STOP SEEKING APPROVAL

Most of us worry excessively about what other people think – which is ironic, because most other people are doing the same thing and are not at all concerned about you. Start living your life on your own terms and accept that, regardless of what you do, there'll be people who don't approve of your choices and even some who don't like you.

Be happy now

How often have you looked into the future and told yourself you'll be happy once you reach a new goal or milestone? Once you lose those last five kilos, get a promotion or change your address. Once you're earning an extra few thousand dollars, have met your ideal partner or when your kids are sleeping through the night.

Then you achieve your goal and find yourself quickly adapting to your new normal. Within a month or two, you're back to feeling that there's just another hurdle to overcome, but you're pretty sure that *this* is the one that will really make you happy.

As I wrote in *Be Mindful & Simplify Your Life*, there's a fascinating concept called 'hedonic adaptation' that describes how we're only content with reaching milestones for a short time before we find ourselves feeling dissatisfied again.

Feeling happier every day involves bringing the power of positive feeling back into the present moment. This doesn't mean you won't have goals, but it does involve learning to be more content with where you are before moving on to the next thing.

Incorporate these tips into your days this week

1. As you travel to work each morning (or, if you're not working at the moment, as you prepare for your day), think of something you're looking forward to that day (having a coffee break mid-morning; seeing a colleague or friend whose company you enjoy; taking your dog for a walk).

2. Let go of unrealistic expectations of how your life should be, and appreciate and feel grateful for what is good in your life right now.

3. Find a couple of attributes in your physical appearance that you're genuinely happy about, and when you look into the mirror each morning remind yourself of these things instead of only focusing on the aspects you don't like.

4. Write down three positive qualities in a friend, a partner, a colleague or a family member who you're finding difficult to get along with at the moment.

5. Grab a pen and paper, and write down at least ten things you have achieved in your life that you feel genuinely proud of. They don't need to be significant achievements – consider small things like being there for a friend when they were in need, getting into the basketball team when you were in school or making it to your yoga class several times this month. Keep the list somewhere you can review it often and add at least one new item each week.

6. Keep your life interesting by continuing to try new things. This is one of the proven factors to improve happiness and one of the best ways to enjoy your every day.

Deal with the Ds

Petrea King, founder and CEO of the Quest for Life Foundation and author of eight books, believes that when we encounter significant obstacles in life, or what she calls 'one of life's Ds', we are suddenly stopped in our tracks and forced to question everything. We may not know how to proceed.

In these moments we realise that what matters is not changing our outer circumstances, but thinking about how we will respond to those circumstances.

ARE YOU DEALING WITH ANY Ds?

Disappointment

Diagnosis

Disaster   Devastation

Debt   Death

Despair   Depression

Drama   Disability

Divorce   Downturn

Drought   Disfigurement

Instead of thinking of such moments as purely negative, consider how many people find suffering to be the very thing that, in Petrea King's words, 'breaks us open to compassion, wisdom and understanding. It is often our suffering that enables us to realise that happiness is not derived from the outer circumstances of our lives – that indeed, happiness is an inside job.'

IF YOU'RE CURRENTLY DEALING WITH ONE OF LIFE'S Ds, THINK OF THE WAYS IT COULD BE A USEFUL OR MEANINGFUL EXPERIENCE.

Allow your negative feelings

From a very young age, most of us were taught to deny our negative feelings. Remember being told to put on a happy face, to control your temper or share your toys (when you really didn't want to)?

When you practise mindfulness, one of the first things you learn is that feelings are just feelings – and none of them are wrong. What's most important is acknowledging everything you feel.

In Tina Gilbertson's book *Constructive Wallowing*, she makes a case for the importance of acknowledging our negative feelings. Most of us naturally acknowledge our positive emotions, but we often try to avoid the negative ones. When we don't acknowledge and allow our negative emotions, we are not truly connecting with ourselves, so it's impossible for us to feel whole.

Our unacknowledged feelings stay trapped inside us and lead to habitual behaviours such as numbing them with food, alcohol, shopping and drugs. The more we stuff those feelings down, the worse we feel about ourselves. Ultimately, unacknowledged feelings can lead to depression, anxiety and a general sense of not being enough.

It's important to make a distinction between acknowledging feelings and acting on them. Allowing for your feelings doesn't mean behaving in reactionary ways – when you acknowledge anger, for example, it doesn't mean you need to yell at someone or even say that you're feeling angry out loud. Even just acknowledging your feelings and having compassion for yourself can create a sense of wholeness that is liberating.

HOW TO FEEL YOUR DIFFICULT FEELINGS

Start by observing what you feel in your body. Is there tightness in your jaw muscles or tension around your eyes? Do you feel any constriction in your chest or belly? Take a couple of breaths and see if you can name the emotion that accompanies that sensation: anger, frustration, irritability, fear, exhaustion, jealousy, sadness?

Let yourself feel the emotion fully and announce to yourself, 'I feel angry,' or, 'I feel frustrated,' or, 'I'm nervous.' Don't immediately push the feeling away – instead, acknowledge its presence. Trying to deny or reject our feelings often exacerbates them. Remind yourself that we all experience these emotions at times.

As well as being fully aware of difficult emotions, notice your desire to reach for the chocolate, wine or your credit card. Instead of behaving habitually, take a moment to pause and think about what's going on. What was it that triggered the feeling?

Have compassion for yourself. It helps to imagine being your own best friend: try saying to yourself, 'This is really hard for you right now, but I am here to take care of you.' At first it might feel a little crazy to talk to yourself like this, but it's one of the greatest techniques you'll ever learn!

If you feel you need to do something proactive in order to deal with a negative emotion, choose an action that aligns with your values, or one that will genuinely help you to feel more at ease (e.g. go for a walk, call a friend, listen to a favourite piece of music, seek the support of a counsellor).

Cultivate compassion

People who are kind to themselves are happier, according to a global study of 16,000 volunteers that was conducted by three German psychologists in 2015.

The researchers identified three key elements to self-compassion. They are:

1. SELF-KINDNESS – cultivating understanding towards yourself in the face of suffering.

2. MINDFULNESS – being aware of how you're feeling without letting any single emotion dominate, not judging your feelings (or yourself) harshly and not seeing a single failing as a reason to believe you're a failure overall.

3. COMMON HUMANITY – seeing our experience as a natural and normal part of the human condition, which reminds us we're not alone in our suffering.

This final element taps into an ancient Buddhist meditation practice called 'Tonglen', sometimes known as the practice of 'giving and receiving'. In Tonglen, we imagine helping others by breathing in the world's suffering and breathing out healing, love and kindness. It might sound like something to leave you feeling pretty deflated and depressed, but in fact it deepens compassion like no other practice and even opens up your capacity for self-compassion. Perhaps counterintuitively, most people say it makes them feel better.

Give it a try

Start by thinking of someone you would love to be able to help. Bring to mind the word or words you would use to describe that person's emotional suffering (e.g. stressed, exhausted, lonely, angry, feeling inadequate, miserable).

On your 'in' breath, imagine you are breathing in their suffering and allow it to open your heart to the truth that others are suffering in the same way. You may even notice that sometimes you suffer in the same way too.

On your 'out' breath, breathe out love, kindness and healing, and imagine that your breath extends to everyone who is suffering in the same way. Feel a deep sense of connection and compassion for others. Let this connectedness also open compassion towards yourself.

9

Accept uncertainty

It's normal to be uncomfortable with uncertainty – nearly everyone is – but sometimes an overly active intolerance of uncertainty exacerbates stress and anxiety, which in turn inhibits our ability to be happy.

Many people deal with uncertainty by trying to create as much certainty as possible. Instead of trying to control everything in your environment, think of uncertainty as a psychological allergy. People who loathe it generally have a strong reaction to it. Try the option of increasing your tolerance of uncertainty.

How to increase your tolerance of uncertainty

- *Name or write down all of your irrational fears.*

- Write down all of the potential outcomes, including the bad ones.

- Write down how you could respond to worst-case scenarios.

- Acknowledge the things that are outside your control.

- Gradually expose yourself to uncertainty to help build resilience (just make sure you do this slowly).

- Challenge your usual behaviours that are designed to control uncertainty (e.g. over-planning, avoidance, procrastination).

Remember that the most likely reason you fear uncertainty is because you're fearful of an unpleasant outcome. Remind yourself that even when bad things happen you will cope with them, and often those are the very experiences that build your resilience.

Don't take it personally

Along the way you're going to encounter someone behaving and talking in a critical or thoughtless way.

Occasionally, criticism will be directed at you in a comment or opinion that's hurtful. Our tendency can be to accept such feedback at face value. We make the assumption that it's valid and accurate, when in fact it may well be far from the truth.

Not all feedback is useful. Consider the following before taking it on board.

- Does the person offering the feedback have similar values to you? Maybe the qualities or characteristics that are important to them barely even matter in your world.

- Is it possible that they have their own stuff going on and are projecting their feelings onto you? For example, people who are insecure are often intimidated by other people's success.

Could you be reading between the lines and making assumptions that are inaccurate? Maybe you think a comment means something other than what it was intended to mean? Maybe you've misinterpreted the tone? Remind yourself that it's always good practice to give people the benefit of the doubt.

ARE YOU BEING TOO SENSITIVE? IF YOU'RE INCLINED TO TAKE THINGS PERSONALLY, ASK YOURSELF WHERE YOU CAN BE MORE IMPARTIAL, AND IF NECESSARY CHECK IN WITH THE PERSON WHO MADE A COMMENT THAT CONCERNED YOU AND ASK THEM (IN A FRIENDLY WAY) IF YOUR INTERPRETATION WAS CORRECT.

Live in the now

Most of us spend a lot of time feeling rushed and distracted. Our minds retreat to the past or worry about the future, and we miss living the moment we're in. Mindfulness can help you live a more conscious and fulfilling life right now.

Try the following tips to help you bring your awareness back to the present.

- Become aware of your breathing. Notice how your body moves as you breathe. Look for where you're holding on to tension in your muscles, and pay attention to your busy thoughts. Say to yourself, 'I'm right here and I'm okay.' As you do, imagine that for now you can just accept everything as it is.

◎ Notice whatever you're experiencing right now –
including emotions, thoughts and physical sensations
– and don't act to change anything. Just be with things
exactly as they are, without any judgement.

◎ Feel your feet on the floor and become aware of your
environment. Notice sounds and people around you
and notice the judgements you make of how things
are 'good' or 'bad', 'positive' or 'negative'. As much as
possible, just allow everything to be as it is. Throughout
your day, repeat this practice for a few minutes at a time.

◎ If you struggle to be mindful, try a short meditation
practice at the beginning of each day. Sit quietly for five
minutes with your eyes closed and pay close attention to
your breathing. If you find it difficult to meditate silently
on your own, download a guided meditation to get you
started. You'll find some links in the resources section at
the end of this book.

(12)

Take back control

Sometimes we feel powerless to change our circumstances, or we have the sense that life is *happening to us* rather than being within our control.

If you have an underlying belief that others are responsible for your happiness, it might be time to get into the driver's seat to take back control of your life.

Review the following statements and identify those you relate to most.

◎ I believe that other people and/or external factors are to blame for my situation.

◎ I feel powerless or helpless to change.

◎ I don't feel like I have choices or options.

- I think other people should be helping me more.

- I complain frequently (but not to those who are the direct source of the problem).

- I sometimes torment myself with negative thinking.

- I resist seeking professional help, preferring instead to complain to friends, work colleagues, family members or partners.

If, hand on heart, any of these statements apply to you, or if you've been feeling or behaving as though you're a passive participant in your life, try the following tips to take back control.

- Change your vocabulary. Instead of using phrases like 'I should' or 'I wish I could', reframe what you are saying to 'I will' or 'I'm going to'.

- Forgive yourself and make a decision to take back control of your life.

- If you're a habitual people-pleaser, practise saying 'no' and learn about how to be more assertive.

Set a few clear but achievable goals and consider the first few action steps you can take to move towards those goals.

Take small steps to build your courage. The most effective way to do this is to scare yourself a little, and a good way to do *that* is by stepping out of what you perceive as your 'comfort zone'. You might find that it wasn't that comfortable after all.

Learn to counter your negative self-talk with a kinder attitude towards yourself.

If you've tried taking positive steps and still can't shake the feeling of being powerless – or if you're feeling constantly unhappy – you may want to seek the support of a professional counsellor or psychologist.

Not where you should be?

Maybe you haven't met your ideal partner and all of your friends are now married and having kids; you might be less senior in your role than your university mates are in theirs; maybe you chose travelling the world over buying property and you now feel like you're locked out of the housing market.

Focusing on what we *haven't* achieved is a certain path to misery. You probably already know that it's demotivating and unhelpful, but it's also difficult to change.

- Make sure you don't escalate negative thinking by gathering evidence that proves you're generally failing. Instead, aim for a more balanced view.

- Make room for any feelings that accompany the sense that you're not where you should be in life, but try not to get caught up in regret. It's helpful to acknowledge your disappointment or discomfort, but it isn't helpful to continue to focus on past mistakes. Those choices are made, so it's time to move on.

Remind yourself of the things you have achieved so far in your life. Most of us skim over or dismiss valuable experiences and achievements, and focus more on what we haven't done so well. Thinking that way is a natural inclination for many of us, but changing it will go a long way to giving you new perspective.

Focus on the future and start being proactive about changing your life for the better. For example, if you really care about meeting a partner, make it a priority and take a few action steps that are likely to move you forward. (And yes, that probably will involve online dating!)

Let go of comparing

We spend a fair amount of our time comparing ourselves to others. For the most part, our comparisons are a combination of favourable and unfavourable judgements. We're constantly sizing people up, which creates a barrier of sorts that inhibits connection.

If you're honest with yourself, you probably believe you're better than some and not as good as others, in many different ways. Maybe you suspect you're not the most clever or beautiful, but you know you have a good sense of humour. You may believe you're more generous than most but less confident and certain. You might think you're more hardworking but less assertive.

Once you start exploring how much you compare, you'll begin to realise that you do it subtly with many aspects of life, not just your personal characteristics.

As important as it is to acknowledge what we're naturally good at (read more about this in *Believe in Yourself & Do What You Love*), we don't want to get caught in the trap of *constantly comparing*. Recognising and proactively engaging your strengths is a positive thing – using them to create distance or make comparisons is not.

HOW ARE YOU COMPARING YOURSELF?

I'M BETTER AT

Humour

Kindness

Empathy

Writing

I'M WORSE AT

Intellect

Assertiveness

Courage

Speaking

HOW ARE YOU THE SAME?

All of us are scared, anxious, embarrassed, vulnerable, intimidated, awkward, jealous and clumsy at times. Just as each of us can be clever, funny, brave, beautiful, kind, loving and articulate too.

Recognise that everyone shares all of the same qualities in different measures, and that we bring them to life in different ways in different situations.

LET GO OF COMPARING; SIMPLY ENJOY YOUR OWN COMPANY WHEN YOU'RE AT YOUR BEST AND CUT YOURSELF SLACK WHEN YOU'RE NOT.

Give of yourself

Think about people in need of a helping hand, whether they are in less developed parts of the world or in your neighbourhood, and consider whatever adversity they are dealing with.

As well as it being a compassionate thing to do, even without taking karma into account, the very act of giving is good for you. It has been proven to contribute to your own sense of self, wellbeing and happiness. The more you're inclined to give (and the more you enjoy giving), the more inclined to generosity you'll be in the future and, as the research has found, the happier you will be.

WHAT'S IN IT FOR YOU?

- Giving promotes positive changes in the brain that are associated with happiness.

- Giving brings about a sense of belonging, making us feel less isolated and alone.

Giving makes life feel more meaningful and reduces negative feelings.

Giving helps keep things in perspective.

Giving even helps us to live longer.

WHERE CAN YOU GIVE?

As the saying goes, charity often begins at home, so start by thinking about how you can give to those who are close by. If you're strapped for time or money, get creative about being generous.

Make an effort to get to know the people who live around you – not so you can live in each other's pockets, but to create a sense of connection with your local community.

Choose a cause that you care about and find out how you can contribute, either financially or by volunteering your time.

Look at volunteering websites where there are flexible options for offering your time (try goodcompany.com.au as a place to start).

(5) Give of yourself

When you're cooking your next meal, make an extra portion to take to a busy friend or an elderly neighbour.

Once a week, make a phone call to a family member or friend who could use your support, even if it's just to listen for half an hour.

Be mindful as you offer to give – not everyone wants to be helped. Sometimes you need to ask permission first.

Make friends with money

Income matters in the pursuit of happiness, but only up to a point.

This has been a consistent finding in the World Happiness Report, an annual survey of 156 countries conducted by Gallup, which has found that beyond a modest living, having more money doesn't make a huge difference to our state of happiness.

The pursuit of wealth for its own sake won't make us happy, but the Gallup findings confirm that feeling a sense of certainty about our finances has a significant impact on our sense of wellbeing.

People who are thriving financially may not be 'rich' by traditional standards. They have enough money to pay their bills, they have money in reserve for emergencies and, importantly, they have a mindset of feeling '*in control*'. Those with financial wellbeing manage their money well, they build financial reserves, they focus on eliminating debt, they spend wisely and they buy experiences rather than material possessions.

People who are less satisfied with their financial situation often avoid thinking about it because they tell themselves they don't have enough money to worry about or they're not hung up about money. Not being properly informed about your money has the potential to keep you trapped in habits (such as over-spending, using credit cards and 'treating yourself' when you really can't afford it) that don't support your long-term financial freedom.

Taking a mindful approach to managing your money can help to diminish worry. As with all aspects of mindful living, it starts with simply being aware. Once you have that awareness, you can begin to make small, manageable changes, which will result in a much greater sense of emotional and financial freedom.

Take time out

When you let yourself get to the point where you're running on empty, you are not much use to anyone and, in fact, you might be a danger to yourself.

When you're overtired, life is more of a strain than it needs to be and things tend to look more negative than they actually are. Each of us needs to manage our energy so that there's always something left in the tank.

If you're one of those people who rarely take a break, start by giving yourself permission to slow down.

1. SCHEDULE REGULAR REST TIMES

Our bodies need rest – and not just the eight hours of sleep we should be aiming for each night. Most busy people baulk at the idea of putting their feet up for fifteen minutes, but a proper rest during the day makes a significant difference to how you feel.

2. AN EARLY NIGHT OR EARLY MORNING

Head to bed at 8.30pm with a book or your favourite mag and leave your phone or tablet out of the bedroom. Try waking at 5am. It's slightly painful at first but once you're up and you've had a cup of tea, you'll be grateful for the time on your own. Write in your journal, watch the sunrise, do a few yoga stretches or meditate.

3. WEEKEND MINI-BREAK

When you're not able to take a two-week trip to Thailand or an extended weekend down the coast, a regular weekend can be transformed into a mini-break.

Nominate a date a few weeks in advance and let people know you won't be available. Keep the time as commitment-free as possible. Spread your usual weekend errands throughout the week before or, better still, just do the basics.

Ask a friend to ferry the kids to sport and order in a few healthy pre-cooked meals. Once Friday night arrives, put your phone on silent and put your feet up. Turn the telly off. Talk to your partner (and not just about the challenging stuff). Take a picnic to the park, walk along the beach, lie on the grass and watch the clouds roll by.

Sometimes it's not a question of whether you can afford the time but whether you can afford not to take the time. Be honest with yourself before you burn out, and everyone will benefit.

Co-operate more

Right from our very early years, we're taught that it's natural to compete.

Mothers in parenting groups compare how well their babies feed and sleep, children as young as five recognise their place in the playground pecking order, and by the time they've finished their first few months at school most kids can tell you the fastest runners in class.

Competing is entrenched in our society. It's in our political systems, corporations and education systems. It's embedded in our psyches, and while many psychologists agree that humans enjoy it, the reality is that competing doesn't necessarily make us happier. It can be a good thing when there's an 'extrinsic incentive' that motivates us to push ourselves harder, and competition is essential in creating markets free from evil monopolies, but it's only good to a point.

When competition motivates us to do better at the same time as building others around us, it's a positive force. But when we rely on it too much, we lose the intrinsic motivation to do well and we're only motivated when there's something to win.

A HEALTHIER APPROACH IS TO VALUE CO-OPERATION AS MUCH AS YOU VALUE COMPETITION. OUR SURVIVAL DEPENDS ON IT, AND WE NEED TO ENSURE WE DON'T LOSE TOUCH WITH THAT.

When we choose not to participate in the rat race (which is, after all, a race that exists only in our heads) or get caught up in what the Joneses are doing, we have more energy for the things that are likely to make us happy.

- Notice when jealousy arises – this is often a precursor to competition.

- Pay attention to the things that other people have or do that cause you to feel a twinge of envy.

Consider how you can move your life more in the direction of what you envy, even if you can't compete.

Be inspired by others' success and let it be a force that pushes you to strive harder, instead of giving up.

Be open-minded

Many of the prejudices we feel as adults developed in childhood when we learned that there are people who belong to 'our group' and those we consider 'others'. Sometimes these differences are subtle enough to be barely noticeable but they often shape the way we connect.

When we encounter someone who is not from our group, we're inclined to be more judgemental and potentially less open-minded. Once we recognise that we all have natural biases, we can watch for how they lead to close-minded or judgemental thinking.

Check in with the list below and add your own (keeping a sense of humour as you do the exercise). Think about how these biases change the way you connect or, indeed, stop you connecting with people and things that could otherwise contribute to your happiness and wellbeing.

WHO DO YOU SEE AS 'OTHERS'?

- People with university degrees

- Uneducated people

- People who eat meat

- Vegetarians

- People who vote for a certain political party

- People who don't understand politics

- People from certain religious groups

- People who don't have a faith

- Non-English speaking people

- People from certain countries

- Australians who are 'ocker'

- Country folk

(19) Be open-minded

◎ City dwellers

◎ People who drive Volvos

◎ People who drive 4WDs

◎ People who've never learned to drive

◎ People who identify as LGBTQIA+

◎ Heterosexual people

◎ People with kids

◎ Married people

◎ Old people

◎ Teenagers

◎ People who watch the ABC

◎ People who watch commercial television

NO DOUBT YOU RECOGNISED
YOURSELF IN MANY OF THOSE
CATEGORIES AND THOUGHT,
'WHY WOULD ANYONE NOT LIKE
ME FOR THAT?'

Know your fears so that you can face them

When you're not entirely happy with your circumstances, you need the courage to try something different. When we consistently avoid things that are daunting, we risk getting so comfortable that we eventually become too afraid to try anything new.

GET CLEAR ABOUT YOUR FEARS AND START FACING THEM

Make a list of all your fears, including the small and irrational ones. For example: I'm afraid of getting sick, I'm afraid of not being good enough, I'm afraid of not having enough money, I'm afraid of making a wrong decision, I'm afraid of being alone.

Once you've made your list, read your fears out loud to yourself (this step is important, so don't skip it just because it feels a bit weird). Allow yourself to feel the fear that comes up without judging yourself for being fearful.

Notice which fears stop you from changing your circumstances and how they hold you back. For example, being afraid of not being good enough might stop you from leaving an unhappy relationship. Being afraid of not having enough money might stop you from looking for a new job.

Choose one fear to face this month. As you'll read in the next chapter, when you're building your capacity for courage, you need to get the balance just right. Take on too big a challenge and you might freeze; take on a task that's not challenging enough and you won't feel motivated to create any kind of change.

Don't get too comfortable

Studies show that we value security over just about anything else in life, which means that we probably tolerate unhealthy or imperfect jobs and relationships for much longer than we really should.

To overcome fear of change, try to value courage as much as security. The key is recognising just the right amount of discomfort to get you moving. As Daniel H Pink says in his book *Drive: The Surprising Truth about What Motivates Us*, 'We need a place of productive discomfort. If you're too comfortable, you're not productive. And if you're too uncomfortable, you're not productive. Like Goldilocks, we can't be too hot or too cold.'

THE EXERCISE

Once you've identified the fear to face this month, choose a couple of clear action steps. Don't make them the most difficult steps to begin with, but be sure you've chosen something that is slightly outside your usual behaviour.

Write down those actions, then choose a specific date and time to take action.

Tell someone what you're planning to do and ask them to hold you accountable. Agree on a time to catch up after you've taken action.

Celebrate. You don't need to throw a party but it's important to take the time to feel proud that you've pushed outside your comfort zone before moving on to the next thing.

Value who you are, not what you do

Many of us define ourselves by the roles we inhabit at work rather than feeling valued for just being who we are. It's one of the reasons many people find retirement so difficult.

Think about the person you are outside of your professional role or the other roles you fulfil as you go through your days. Who are you without the label of worker, student, mother, sister, daughter, son or carer? What would people say about you, simply for being the person you are? How do you want to think of yourself? What kind of person do you want to be?

WHO ARE YOU OUTSIDE OF YOUR USUAL ROLES?

- A generous friend

- A good listener

- Someone who makes people laugh

- An advocate for those in need

- A calming influence

- A good decision-maker

- Someone with an adventurous spirit

- A person who loves sharing ideas

- Someone wise and insightful

- A person who has the courage to challenge the status quo

Choose the values from the list that resonate, add others that are dear to you and redouble your efforts to actually live these qualities out.

Write your way to a solution

Our brains function differently when we write things down. In fact, writing can have a similar effect on the brain to meditation. Our breathing slows and, unless we're being critical of our work, the act of writing helps to create a sense of calm.

One form of writing that evokes such a state is stream-of-consciousness writing, and it can drastically reduce stress levels.

Julia Cameron, author of the much-loved book *The Artist's Way* (first published almost twenty-five years ago), recommends a practice called 'morning pages' where, on waking, you write three pages about anything that enters your mind. The writing doesn't need to be quality – you don't need to show this to anyone or even read it again yourself – it's simply about making contact with your thoughts to help you better understand yourself.

There are added benefits too. Free-form writing like this helps expose the inner critic, clears the mind, reduces anxiety and, ultimately, enhances creativity. As Cameron says, writing morning pages helps you to become acquainted with all of the dark corners of your psyche, and when you put that negativity on the page, it isn't eddying through your consciousness during the day.

GIVE IT A TRY

- Set your alarm thirty minutes earlier than usual and have a pen (or pencil) and paper ready.

- Write by hand, don't type. The reason for this is that free-hand writing is slower than typing, and this extra time helps you to make contact with your inner world.

- Write about whatever you like. If you're stuck, write: 'I'm stuck. I have no idea what to write, I should be getting on with my day,' is fine to begin with. Just keep going and trust the process. You'll be surprised at how it eventually feels as though the pages start to write themselves.

Focus on life's positives

One inhibitor of happiness is our tendency to focus on the negative aspects of life. When we watch the news it's hard not to be concerned because we're constantly served up stories about how terrible the world is. But we see less than half the real story.

Media stories add to our brain's natural tendency towards negativity, and they often lead to worrying about circumstances that we're not in a position to change. While it's important to choose a couple of causes that you can proactively support or advocate for, taking all that worry on board can be deeply disheartening and unproductive.

To obtain a balanced view, you should also seek out stories about what's good in the world.

- Follow positive news websites (try the Positive News or Good News Network sites).

- Become someone who shares positive stories with others.

- Actively choose a couple of causes that you want to support, and do your best to focus on those while trying not to overthink all of the other problems in the world.

- Set aside news-free days at least twice a week.

Focus on your positives

Our natural inclination is to find fault with ourselves instead of focusing on our positive characteristics. This biased view becomes problematic when our inner critic works overtime.

Focusing on your flaws drains your energy, has a negative impact on your mood and often makes you less enjoyable company for others.

It takes a strong will and concerted effort to look for the good in ourselves. It helps if we recognise that this is not simply an exercise in self-indulgence. There's an upside for the people around you too – when you're not as busy worrying about yourself, you'll be more present and connected with others.

◎ Familiarise yourself with the 'broken record' thoughts you have about yourself that are self-critical. Consider how you think about your physical appearance, your intelligence, the work you do, the kind of person you are, the relationships you have. Write down all of the critical thoughts you can think of. It might sound like a negative exercise, but once you see your criticisms in black and white you may get a shock at how hard you are on yourself, which can open you up to more self-compassion.

◎ PUT AN ASTERISK NEXT TO THE AREAS YOU CAN GENUINELY CHANGE. BE REALISTIC HERE. IT MAY NOT BE POSSIBLE TO DRAMATICALLY ALTER YOUR PHYSICAL APPEARANCE OR THE KIND OF PERSON YOU ARE, BUT THERE MAY BE SMALL ASPECTS OF YOURSELF THAT CAN BE ADJUSTED WITH A BIT OF EFFORT.

○ Think about how you can move towards something that's a *slight improvement*, but not perfect. For example, if you don't love your appearance, consider how you can make the best of your good features. Maybe there's a colour you look great in or an outfit that makes you feel attractive.

○ When you're in the company of others, notice how much more engaged you are when you focus less on your flaws. Instead of having an experience where you're listening to the chatter inside your head, be fully present with whoever you're talking to.

Look for the good in others

Now that you've noticed the strong negative bias of the brain, spend the next twenty-four hours catching your critical thoughts about other people.

Begin with those closest to you and work your way outwards. Notice even the smallest of irritations, like a partner who leaves their clothes on the floor, the messy housemate, whiny kids, neighbours who play their music too loudly or the colleague who just doesn't seem to stop talking.

 Do your best to counter criticism with tolerance and acceptance by considering how some of your habits might be annoying for others. This is not intended as an exercise in self-criticism, but rather a way of finding a more balanced perspective.

◎ REMIND YOURSELF THAT
WHEN YOU BECOME OVERLY
FOCUSED ON HOW PEOPLE ARE
IRRITATING YOU, THERE'S LITTLE
ROOM TO REMEMBER WHAT
YOU LIKE ABOUT THESE PEOPLE.

◎ Shift your focus for a day (or several days) to proactively remind yourself of what you love (or at least like) about the same people. Maybe your partner is messy but kind; maybe your kids are whiny but fun. Maybe your chatty colleague is a breath of fresh air in an otherwise serious workplace.

Worry less

Worry is a natural part of life and a useful tool to keep us safe from risk. While we're all inclined to worry from time to time, some of us are serious worrywarts and that does us no good at all.

If you find yourself constantly seeking out new things to worry about, try this cognitive-behavioural therapy technique as a means of quelling your concerns.

Set aside thirty minutes in the morning or at the end of your workday as 'worry time' (ideally don't make it right before bedtime). This chunk of time is scheduled for the sole purpose of checking in with the things that are causing you to feel anxious or concerned. When you first attempt the 'worry time' activity, you might find that it feels difficult or even counterintuitive. With practice, it helps to contain an overly active worrying mind.

FIVE STEPS TO 'WORRY TIME':

1. Set aside fifteen to thirty minutes each day for worry time and schedule it into your diary.

2. When you become aware of unnecessary worrying thoughts during your day, acknowledge those thoughts and do your best to consciously set them aside until your worry time.

3. During your worry time, write down all of your worrying thoughts. It's therapeutic to bring your worries out into the open and to properly examine them, rather than leaving them in the background gnawing away at your sense of ease and happiness. The exercise helps to give you a greater perspective.

4. You may find it helpful to begin to explore potential solutions to your main concerns and identify small action steps that you can easily take to progress those solutions, but this is not the main objective of worry time.

5. Pay attention to habitual worries – most of us find we get fixed on a set of concerns that repeatedly go around in our heads.

Be more optimistic

Research has found that optimism has benefits for your health and happiness, which can lead to a longer life. Not only that, but also people are drawn to optimists, and there's even evidence that optimism can make you luckier and more successful (particularly if you work in sales).

If you think you're naturally predisposed to pessimism and there's nothing anyone can do about it, think again. According to Martin Seligman, author of *Learned Optimism*, the first thing to do is learn where your pessimism comes from. He suggests that it's largely about your 'explanatory style', i.e. what you tell yourself when things go wrong.

There are three key areas to watch for – permanence, pervasiveness and personalisation.

PERMANENCE

Optimists think, 'I'm feeling unmotivated,' while pessimists interpret the same mood as 'I'm a lazy and hopeless person.' Recognise that bad things don't last forever.

PERVASIVENESS

Optimists limit negative thinking to the specifics, while pessimists are prone to making them universal. For example, 'My boss is in a grumpy mood today,' can become, 'Everyone at my workplace is always in a bad mood.'

PERSONALISATION

And finally, a more positive approach is about making things less personal. In other words, thinking, 'I don't fully understand this software,' as opposed to 'I'm completely useless with IT.'

Optimists recognise that bad things are temporary, that they generally have a specific cause and that they happen to all of us.

TRAIN YOURSELF TO BE MORE OPTIMISTIC

Next time you're having a tough day, notice how the story goes in your head. Check your 'explanatory style'.

Are you saying things to yourself that sound permanent and pervasive? Are you blaming yourself fully rather than accepting that it's not your fault if you're having a bad day?

Pessimists recognise that happiness is fleeting, but they often miss the moment because they're thinking that when it disappears, it will never return.

OPTIMISTS RECOGNISE THAT HAPPINESS IS FLEETING, BUT THEY SAVOUR THE MOMENT AND KNOW IT WILL BE BACK.

When you notice negative thinking, change permanent explanations to less permanent ones, change pervasive explanations to specific ones and change personal blame to a more general perspective.

(29)

Balance your optimism

While being optimistic has a positive impact on how happy you are, it's important not to let it get out of hand.

Extreme optimists believe that everything will be rosy – always and in all areas of their lives. They don't plan for things to go wrong, and they overestimate how healthy and successful they'll be.

Denmark consistently rates as the happiest nation in the world, according to the annual World Happiness reports, and that's partly because the Danes are particularly good at keeping a balanced perspective. The theory goes that because they don't expect great things to happen all the time, when anything slightly above average occurs they feel a significant boost to their moods.

Anticipating too much happiness can deprive you of the satisfaction of small pleasures, but that's not the only downside of extreme optimism. According to a 2007 report by Manju Puri and David Robinson, professors of finance at Duke University in the United States, extreme optimists take bigger financial risks, save less money and often overestimate how healthy they'll be, so are less cautious in general.

Being overly optimistic can lead you to ignore small problems (which can eventually lead to bigger problems). When you find yourself being positive about everything and never wanting to look at the negatives, consider balancing your thoughts by looking at a situation from all angles – and occasionally asking yourself, 'What might go wrong here?'

Define your own happiness

If you accept that not comparing yourself to others is key to being happier – and hopefully you will – then it stands to reason that you shouldn't compare your *idea* of happiness to someone else's idea, or even what the majority's idea of what happiness might be.

No one can decide what will truly fulfil another, and it's up to each of us to define where genuine and lasting contentment resides. Defining your own version of happiness means disconnecting from the mainstream and working out how to live *your* best life.

THE EXERCISE

Grab your journal and spend the next ten minutes answering the following questions.

- Who would you be if you stopped worrying about what other people think?

- If you were granted a wish for the one personal attribute you need to fulfil your dreams, what would it be?

- What would you do with your life if you had no fear of failing and no need to make an income?

- What relationships do you need to be genuinely fulfilled (include the attributes of those people too)?

◎ What's missing from your life right now?

◎ What is one lasting impact that you would like to make on the world?

31

Discover your purpose

Viktor Frankl was an Austrian neurologist and psychiatrist who survived three years in concentration camps and went on to write the bestselling book *Man's Search for Meaning*.

Frankl rarely wrote about the pursuit of happiness, but he had a determined interest in how purpose can give us something to feel positive about and provide fulfilment.

Frankl believed we should set our sights on finding our reasons to live, not on pursuing happiness for the sake of it.

Defining your purpose begins with learning about yourself and considering the contribution you want to make to others.

Try not to limit yourself by deciding that your purpose has to be about your career. Consider the following questions in relation to all areas of your life.

What are your unique gifts?

How can you use your gifts to make a difference in other people's lives, every day?

What are you passionate about? (Or if 'passionate' sounds like too big a word, what are you genuinely interested in?) Consider the articles you're drawn to in newspapers and magazines, conversations you'd like to be part of, and world issues that concern you most.

What would you want to do with your time, even if you weren't getting paid for it?

Who are the people you most want to help? This can be those in your immediate circle as well as individuals or groups in the greater community.

Is there a legacy you'd like to leave behind?

How do you want to be remembered?

Ask yourself, 'What can I do with my life that will really matter?'

Write down your dreams

Sometimes we have our dreams floating around in our subconscious, but we're not brave enough to put them out in the world by writing them down because we fear they might not be possible to achieve.

While it's true that a goal of meeting your ideal partner within the next twelve months might not be entirely within your control, without intentional action (going on dates etc.) it's a lot less likely to happen.

Writing down your dreams is the first step to making them real.

START WITH YOUR VISION

Set aside an afternoon to daydream about your version of a beautiful life, and then write down your vision for five years from now. Write in the present tense, as though it's real, and cover as many areas as you can.

THINK ABOUT WHERE YOU'D BE LIVING, YOUR IDEAL HOME, WHAT YOU'D BE DOING FOR WORK, HOW YOUR RELATIONSHIPS WOULD LOOK, HOW YOU'D BE TAKING CARE OF YOUR HEALTH AND WELLBEING.

List the qualities of your 'best possible self': are you confident, creative and kind? Clever, witty and adventurous? Gentle, thoughtful and nurturing? Or something different altogether?

Try not to get bogged down in making it perfect. While you're aiming for a life that inspires you, it's useful to acknowledge that your version of an ideal life will most likely involve some compromise.

NOW SET SOME GOALS

Once you've written out your vision, make a list of a few goals you'll need to achieve in the next twelve months that will move you towards that dream.

The most effective way of setting goals is to make them specific, measurable and time-framed. Let's say your vision includes starting your own business: the first goal might be to research small business courses this month, and the second goal might be to complete a course within the next twelve months.

If you're currently single and you have a goal of sharing your life with a partner, your goal might be to join an online dating service within the next two weeks (don't leave it so long that you lose your nerve!) and then to go on at least one date a week.

Seek inspiration

While the pursuit of happiness requires us to draw on our inner resources, we can also benefit from looking outward. Even if you're highly self-motivated, you'll benefit from being inspired by the world and people around you.

Inspiration comes in many forms – think of it as anything that awakens emotion within you or invites you to think differently.

Next time you feel like you've lost your spark, try these tips.

- Read a biography. Choose a story about someone overcoming adversity.

- Book a holiday to somewhere off the beaten track, and allow yourself to be completely inspired by the natural world.

Hang out with a child for an afternoon and look at the world the way they do.

Watch a TED Talk.

People watch. Find a cafe in a busy place, sit by the window and watch the world go by. Observe how people dress, talk, walk and interact with one another. Be curious about their stories, their dreams and the kind of people they are.

Explore spirituality. This doesn't mean you need to be religious: you can just take an interest in the simple rituals that give meaning to so many others – activities like meditation, singing, practising gratitude, spending time 'unplugged', giving of yourself and abstaining from certain habits for a day or two. Do all of these things with an open and inquisitive mind.

Let go of the past

The struggles of childhood and our teenage years often stay with us well into our adult life (and sometimes even right til the end of our days). While genuine trauma has a lasting impact, many of our childhood afflictions are avoidable burdens that hold us back from living in peace.

Sometimes old struggles keep humming away in the background, and we're not conscious of how they play out in current relationships or how they inhibit our capacity for success.

If you know you're carrying a few demons from earlier years, it might be liberating to spend a dozen or so sessions with a good therapist to make sense of how these things affect you now.

Even if your younger years were relatively stress-free, you still may find there are limiting thoughts that you can attribute to a years-old comment or behaviour by a teacher, parent or friend.

Spend some time over the coming days thinking about how old thought patterns limit you. You might discover that they're no longer relevant.

THOUGHT: 'This new activity will be uncomfortable.'

USUAL BEHAVIOUR: Not trying new things, staying in your comfort zone.

THE CHALLENGE: As long as it's not life-threatening or illegal, try it anyway.

THOUGHT: 'I'm not great in new social settings.'

USUAL BEHAVIOUR: Declining invitations, not reaching out to

make new friends, not being open when others reach out to you.

THE CHALLENGE: Observe how others handle themselves in new situations and 'adopt' some of their behaviour. Shake off the old version of you – sometimes it's all in your mindset.

THOUGHT: 'I'll probably get this wrong.'

USUAL BEHAVIOUR: Being defensive, being overly anxious (which means you're even more likely to make an error).

THE CHALLENGE: Reframe your thinking as best you can to, 'If I'm focused and positive, I'm more likely to get this right,' and give it your best shot. If you make a mistake, be gracious about it, rather than defensive.

Be your best self

Each of us can imagine a version of ourselves that we might call our 'best possible selves'. We may have experienced hours (or if we're lucky, days or weeks) where we have been at our best.

But more often than not, even when we experience glimpses of our optimum selves, they're difficult to sustain.

While being mindful not to get caught in perfectionistic behaviour, set your intention to move closer to your version of the best possible you. It usually helps to do this incrementally rather than trying to overhaul your personality or habits overnight.

Use the following tips as a guide.

- Withhold criticism or complaints for an entire day.

- As you start your day, make a connection with the most confident part of you and set an intention to bring this part to life. One way to do this is to close your eyes for a few moments and imagine yourself as a person who walks and talks with confidence – someone who is able to put aside self-doubt and feels a sense of certainty about who they are.

Connect with the calm, grounded part of yourself by taking three deep breaths before responding when you feel frustrated or angry.

Discover the generous part of yourself by putting someone else's needs ahead of yours once every day for the next week.

Let go of your arrogant, egotistical or defensive sides by giving yourself permission to be wrong sometimes (and owning up to that).

Give up blaming others or being a martyr by always putting your own needs last. Take responsibility for your own happiness.

Look for the good in every situation and person you encounter.

Develop your grit

According to University of Pennsylvania psychologist Angela Lee Duckworth, 'grit' (or, in other words, the talent for hard work and persistence) is one of the most predictive variables of success.

Duckworth describes grit as having passion and perseverance for long-term goals, and having the stamina to stick with your plans for the future.

If you doubt whether you have much capacity for grit, consider the fact that you can develop it by engaging the following characteristics.

1. COURAGE

Courageous people take chances where others won't, they stand up for what they believe (particularly when their beliefs are unpopular) and they are able to say 'no' when necessary.

2. CONSCIENTIOUSNESS

Conscientious people generally have strong moral principles and values. They like to do things the right way and do them well. They're dedicated to working hard and capable of a single-minded focus. They generally like being organised and working in tidy spaces.

3. PERSEVERANCE

Those with perseverance are the ones who start on a path and continue towards a purposeful goal. They stick with their goals even when the going gets tough.

4. RESILIENCE

Resilience is the capacity to bounce back from adversity. For the most part, optimistic people are good at resilience. They define their own version of success and they're able to laugh at themselves when they make mistakes. Importantly, they ride the waves of life and cultivate a mindful approach to the ups and downs.

5. PASSION AND PURPOSE

It's easier to be 'gritty' when you choose goals that align with your passions and a deep sense of purpose. It also helps to know your values and beliefs, and to live in alignment with them.

A healthier approach to your health

If you've spent years beating yourself up for not going to the gym or for including sugar, wine or Friday-night takeaway in your diet, maybe it's time to let that go and create a more balanced approach to healthy living.

Do what feels good to you. Listen to your body. Be realistic about your body type and your natural size. Recognise that much of what you hear about how to take better care of your body is conflicting and sometimes even unhelpful. In Rick Kausman's book *If Not Dieting, Then What?* you'll find lots of sensible advice, including some of the following.

 Get rid of the idea of 'good' and 'bad' foods. Instead,

categorise foods as 'everyday' and 'sometimes'. When you do choose a 'sometimes' food, give yourself permission to thoroughly enjoy it.

- Give up 'dieting' and counting calories forever.

- Incorporate plenty of vegetables and natural grains into your meal plans and eat foods as close to the natural source wherever possible.

- Develop a friendly relationship with food rather than treating it like the enemy.

- Tune in to your body and learn to recognise hunger. Eat when you're genuinely hungry rather than to soothe your emotions. Enjoy your food and only eat until you're 80 per cent full – your body will take a while to register what you've eaten.

- Make a list of activities that soothe you emotionally and that don't involve eating. These might include taking a bath, meeting a friend for coffee (or herbal tea), journalling, walking in the park, having a massage or doing something creative.

◎ Be gentle with yourself when you notice the desire to eat emotionally. Be aware of what you're doing and recognise the emotions you feel. If you decide that this is what you need for now, tell yourself, 'I'm eating for comfort and I give myself permission to do this.' The more mindful you are about your behaviour, the easier it will be to choose soothing alternatives.

◎ Tune in to your body one hour after eating so you get to know which foods make you feel energised or lethargic. Make choices about what you eat based on this information.

◎ Move your body more, but in a way that feels pleasurable. Give up the idea that you'll get to the gym or go for a run if you actually loathe it – do something you enjoy instead.

◎ Notice your best natural features and get in the habit of complimenting yourself. You don't have to look in the mirror and say, 'You're gorgeous,' (though you can, and it *will* improve your self-image) but learn to be a little kinder to yourself.

If you have anyone in your life who makes unsupportive comments about your physical appearance, let them know that this needs to stop immediately. Be assertive, not aggressive, but make it clear that it's not appropriate.

Learn to meditate so that you're more in tune with your body and your physical needs.

Change the way you think about taking care of your health – make a choice to treat your body with respect because *you value yourself* and want to feel more energised today, tomorrow and well into the future, rather than making choices based on a need to be perfect.

Have a laugh

You may not be a natural comedian, but you can still embrace and enjoy the benefits of humour throughout your day.

If you don't feel like you're inherently funny, try the following to help you laugh a little more at life. And if you are funny, remember to look at the funny side of things even more often.

- Learn to laugh at yourself.

- Seek out funny stories. Follow comedians on social media and ask friends to share funny stories, videos or books.

- Learn about your own sense of humour. What are the things that amuse you most?

- Practise being witty, but don't try too hard. It helps to find a role model who does this in a way that appeals to you.

○ Be mindful of what sort of humour is appropriate where and when. Find a few different ways to be funny so you can avoid offending people.

○ Look for the humorous side in difficult scenarios.

○ KEEP IT KIND. SARCASM OR LAUGHING AT OTHER PEOPLE'S EXPENSE MIGHT GET A LAUGH, BUT CONSIDER THE UNDERLYING INTENTION. CLEVER HUMOUR IS CONSIDERATE OF OTHERS.

○ Don't take things so seriously in general.

(39)

Look for the good

According to world-renowned author and couples expert Dr John Gottman, our relationships will generally be as good as we make them. In stable, happy relationships, Gottman found, the ratio of positive to negative interactions is 5:1, whereas in relationships heading for divorce the ratio is most likely 0:8.

Essentially, the difference implies that we need to learn to interact in a more positive way if we want our relationships to thrive.

One of the key factors Gottman raises is the issue of criticism. We need to recognise that criticising partners is different to offering feedback.

FEEDBACK IS HELPFUL AND
GENERALLY RELATED TO SPECIFIC
ISSUES, WHILE CRITICISM IS MORE
OFTEN PERCEIVED AS A PERSONAL
ATTACK.

Critical people often convince themselves that they're just giving others helpful feedback. Here are some ways to tell the two apart.

Criticism focuses on what's wrong while feedback focuses on how to improve.

CRITICISM: *Why don't you ever help around the house?*

FEEDBACK: *We need to work out a schedule for taking care of the housework together.*

Criticism is about the other's personality while feedback is about the behaviour.

CRITICISM: You're lazy and unhelpful.

FEEDBACK: Can we start by choosing which tasks each of us are happy to take on?

Criticism implies blame while feedback focuses on resolving the problem.

CRITICISM: It's your fault our house is always a mess.

FEEDBACK: We can get out of this mess if we both chip in. Where do you think we should start?

Criticism is controlling while feedback is respectful of different points of view.

CRITICISM: I'm smarter than you and I know what's best.

FEEDBACK: I respect your decision, even though I don't agree with it.

Release blame

Occasionally, people will act in ways that have a negative impact on you. Our tendency when we've been slighted is to apportion blame and ruminate over all of the ways that the other person is wrong.

Assigning blame isn't empowering. It manifests negativity and robs you of the feeling that you're in charge of your own life. Taking responsibility for your choices and your responses in difficult circumstances allows you to reclaim your strength. It also serves as a reminder that you're capable of standing up for yourself when people treat you poorly.

Breaking our habit of blaming others is only one part of the reclamation of power. Forgiveness also plays an important role. When people hurt you, remind yourself that they may not have done it intentionally. Forgiving them doesn't make what they did okay, but it will free you from the toxic effects of continued blame.

Release yourself from the blame game by trying these steps.

◎ Over the next few days, catch yourself as you assign blame to other people. The easiest way to do this is to watch your language – discover all of the ways you essentially tell yourself that someone else is responsible for your mood, your performance or your wellbeing.

◎ Remind yourself that often a situation has several contributing factors and there's a chance you may also have played a part in how things panned out. Try not to blame yourself, but recognise your contribution and remind yourself that everyone was doing their best.

◎ Instead of looking for who is to blame, focus on narrowing down the real problem and identifying the best options to move forward.

◎ Give others the benefit of the doubt and don't assume you know what they are thinking.

Be spiritual in your own way

Being spiritual doesn't mean signing up to a particular religion or way of thinking, but rather imbuing your days with some deeper meaning. If you don't feel spiritual but would like to, try the following tips to get you started.

CREATE A MORNING RITUAL

Ritual is often helpful in a spiritual practice. It can make us feel more centred and calm, which is particularly useful during difficult times. Start your day with a short morning ritual to get you into a positive frame of mind. Include anything that makes you feel grounded – try a gratitude practice or five minutes of deep breathing before getting out of bed; consider a short walk every morning (regardless of the weather) or fifteen minutes of yoga to wake up your body.

If you're easing your way into spirituality, you might prefer to start with the simple ritual of enjoying a quiet cup of tea before you tackle your day. If you're a parent, teach your kids that these few minutes are yours alone – it won't take long before they catch on.

CONNECT WITH WHO YOU ULTIMATELY WANT TO BE

Set aside an hour to consider what a meaningful life is to you. What is it right now, and what might it be in the future? Having a sense that you're moving in the direction of the things that matter is a key element in a spiritual practice. It gives you the sense that you're living for something bigger than just yourself.

PRACTISE KINDNESS

Giving without the expectation of receiving anything in return is a practice in spirituality. Share your time, your knowledge, your skills, or give financially to someone in need. Listen and allow space for a friend to talk; practise patience with a colleague or family member who frustrates you. Find conscious ways to make small offerings in your relationships every day.

APPRECIATE SYNCHRONICITY

Have you ever learned of a new concept and then had that same concept appear in your life three times in the following week? Or mentioned something obscure to a friend and had them tell you that they were thinking of exactly the same thing? These events are what we call 'synchronicity', and many spiritual people believe they occur when we're on our true path in life. Learn to look for and appreciate experiences where synchronicity appears – even if you don't believe there's anything to it other than pure coincidence. It's a fascinating idea.

Embrace creativity

Connecting with creativity is another great way to feel happier. The stimulation we feel when we are being creative can alleviate stress, reduce depression and improve our sense of wellbeing and self-worth. Practising some form of art can even help us deal with chronic illness.

Being creative brings us more into the present moment, allows us to feel and process our emotions more effectively, and is just plain enjoyable (as long as we're not being overly perfectionist about it). A recent study at the University of London found that even viewing art can increase the activity in the brain's frontal cortex, resulting in a boost in dopamine and feelings of pleasure.

Keith Sawyer, research psychologist and author of *Zig Zag: The Surprising Path to Greater Creativity*, recommends

the following exercises to help open up your capacity
for creativity.

ASK

Write ten versions of the same question. For example, if
you're thinking, 'Where should I go on holiday?' you might
write, 'How can I feel more relaxed? What kind of holiday do
I need right now? How can I make my weekends feel more
like a mini-break?' Your new questions will get you thinking in
a different way.

LEARN

Fill your mind with a variety of information. Seek out
knowledge from nature, art, philosophy, mentors, music,
websites and magazines, as well as formal classrooms.

THINK

Set aside 'ideas time' when you're not distracted by other
activities. Try a few different methods to stimulate creative
thinking such as listing unusual uses for a paper clip, a rubber
band, or a length of string. Give yourself five minutes to

come up with as many ideas as you can (even crazy ones – this is not about logical thinking, it's about opening up your capacity for thinking outside the box).

FUSE

Learn to combine ideas by making random associations. For example, go to page twenty in two different books and choose the first word on the tenth line in each book, then create a poem, a story or a piece of art that makes use of both of those words.

MAKE

Make your ideas visible by drawing a picture (even if you're terrible at drawing). If drawing feels like too much of a stretch, create a collage by cutting out images from magazines or downloading photos online and dragging them into a PowerPoint document.

(43)

Embrace small pleasures

Sometimes we overlook the fact that even during the most difficult times, we can nurture ourselves by embracing small pleasures.

Make a list of the small ways you can create beauty and bring greater nourishment into your life straight away.

- *Eat and savour beautiful food every day.*

- *Make your living spaces appealing.*

- *Handwrite a letter to brighten someone else's day.*

◎ Sleep in on a rainy morning.

◎ Listen to music without other distractions.

◎ Buy a book.

◎ Spend time in nature every day.

◎ Seek out sunshine.

◎ Light a candle.

◎ Go for a swim.

◎ Buy yourself flowers.

◎ Take a bath.

◎ Read for pleasure.

◎ Give someone a long hug.

◎ Do something creative.

Relax your body

When you're feeling anxious your body releases stress hormones into the bloodstream, and these hormones make you physically (and mentally) more uptight. Carrying around physical tension can become habitual, even when we're not particularly stressed.

One of the most effective ways to defuse stress is to tune in to the body on a regular basis and make a habit of learning to physically relax.

Try these research-based behaviours to get you started.

BREATHE DEEPLY

Deep breathing (i.e. from the diaphragm) helps to engage the parasympathetic nervous system, calming down the 'fight or flight' response that is activated when we feel stressed.

LISTEN TO MUSIC

Classical music, particularly the relaxing kind, has a soothing effect on your body, reducing your heart rate, lowering blood pressure and reducing stress hormones. But researchers say that *all* kinds of music can soothe anxiety and boost your mood (with the possible exception of heavy metal).

USE A GUIDED BODY SCAN MEDITATION

Listen to a guided body scan meditation, which will help you to be more aware of your usual tension spots and make it easier to relax. You'll find lots of these online, or you could try my version on the Insight Timer app, which is available for free.

INDULGE IN THE POWER OF TOUCH

There are so many physical benefits to getting a massage: physical touch can boost your general outlook on life, reduce stress and anxiety, improve your balance and increase your range of motion. While getting a massage might feel like an indulgence, it's equally good medicine.

HUG

Hugging is said to increase oxytocin, a hormone that helps to decrease stress and heal feelings of loneliness and isolation.

IF THERE'S NO ONE AROUND WHO NEEDS A HUG RIGHT NOW, YOU COULD EVEN TRY A SELF-HUG (CROSSING YOUR ARMS AROUND YOUR CHEST).

It's said to confuse the brain and provide a sense of comfort and safety, reducing the nervous system's reactivity to stress.

Choose your attitude

There are plenty of things we have no power over in our lives, but the one thing we *do* choose is the attitude we bring to our day.

Regardless of what's going on around you, think about the person you want to be. What kind of attitude do you want to bring to the different situations that you find yourself in throughout your day?

AT THE START OF THE DAY

Before you leave the house, take a moment to check how you're feeling and whether or not you're satisfied with that. If not, choose a word or a phrase that describes how you want to approach your day. For example, if you're feeling irritable, choose 'calm'. If you're feeling negative, try 'grateful'. If you're generally worn down by life, try a more energised approach and see if it makes a difference.

THROUGHOUT YOUR DAY

When you're not enjoying your work, it's tempting to give yourself permission to bring a grumpy attitude to the office. Remind yourself that this reflects on the way you're perceived but also how you feel about yourself. Always adopt a professional approach at work, regardless of your mood.

WITH EXTENDED FAMILY

Many of us have at least one member of our extended family with whom we would happily spend less time. Avoid getting caught up in behaving badly when you're with that person. Actively choose an *adult approach* each time you're in their company.

AT THE END OF THE DAY

Leave behind the negativity of your workday, particularly if you're heading home to others. If you genuinely feel you need to vent before immersing yourself in your 'home time', create an agreement with your partner that each of you has five minutes of complaining time before moving on to a more positive way of interacting.

Practise gratitude

There's growing awareness that developing a regular habit of practising gratitude has effects that will reverberate through your entire life.

BEING THANKFUL IMPROVES YOUR PHYSICAL HEALTH. People who feel grateful experience fewer physical ailments than others, and they generally take better care of their health. One study found that they even sleep better.

GRATITUDE IMPROVES EMPATHY, REDUCES AGGRESSION AND CAN ULTIMATELY HELP IMPROVE YOUR RELATIONSHIPS. In a study conducted by the University of Kentucky, participants with higher gratitude scores tended to behave with sensitivity and empathy, even when given negative feedback.

 Practise gratitude

BEING THANKFUL BOOSTS YOUR EMOTIONAL WELLBEING. Toxic emotions such as regret, envy, frustration, fear and shame are reduced when we feel grateful.

GRATITUDE MULTIPLIES. Taking the time to recognise and be thankful for the positive things and people in your life actually increases the number of positive things and people in your life.

A FEW SIMPLE WAYS TO PRACTISE GRATITUDE

- On waking, think of three things you're grateful for.

- At the end of each day, share with your housemates, partner or children something that went well during your day. If you live alone, write it in your journal.

- Start a gratitude list and add one thing to it every day.

(47)

Embrace change

It's too easy to stay tucked up in what we think is our comfort zone, and we all make excuses for why we can't proactively create change in our lives, even though we know deep in our hearts that we need it.

We tell ourselves, 'I don't want to rock the boat,' 'I don't want people to think badly of me,' 'I don't want to make a mistake,' 'It's too risky,' or 'I have no influence over this.' We make our excuses and then wait for our life to improve by itself. Some situations aren't easy to change, but many are. Embracing change means claiming back your power and your energy.

We might assume that the people who take charge of their lives are assertive and filled with self-belief, but not everyone feels completely confident when they set out to create change. If you're a little fearful, you just need to think it through clearly, make sound decisions and take the first step.

(47) Embrace change

○ **START DOING INSTEAD OF DREAMING.**
Don't just talk about your dreams. Put a plan into action to set up a business, take a trip or start writing a blog. Remember, the first step is often the most important.

○ **DEMONSTRATE THAT YOU'RE CAPABLE.**
If you're seeking to advance your career, don't be afraid to demonstrate your abilities at work. Note your achievements. Make a meeting time with your boss and point out that you'd be comfortable performing a more senior role and you'd like to be considered for promotion when the opportunity arises.

○ **OPEN UP A DISCUSSION.** Instead of waiting for someone else to start the conversation (even if it's a difficult one), be brave enough to go there.

○ **SHOW UP AND BE YOURSELF.** Stop selling yourself short by adapting who you are to fit in with the people you're with. Be yourself in every situation.

◎ **SLOW DOWN**. If you're exhausting yourself by constantly taking on too much or not setting boundaries, consider how you can create more balance.

◎ **NOURISH YOUR MIND AND BODY**. Take better care of yourself with healthy food, exercise and meditation to improve your energy levels. Be mindful of what you can enjoy in your life right now.

Increase your emotional energy

The number of hours you work and the amount of sleep you get are not the only significant influences on your energy levels: your emotional wellbeing also plays a big part.

If you're feeling unhappy, it stands to reason that you're not going to have much zest for life. But if you change how you think and open yourself up to feeling happier now, you're much more likely to have a spring in your step.

Make sure you're eating the right foods, getting enough exercise and taking care of your wellbeing in all of the obvious ways, but also try the following suggestions to boost your energy levels.

1. STAND UP FOR YOURSELF

If you find that you feel powerless in certain relationships, learn to stand up for yourself in a calm and assertive way.

2. SPEND LESS TIME WITH NEGATIVE PEOPLE

Become aware of the relationships that leave you feeling drained or depleted, and either spend less time with those people or move away from them completely.

3. CONNECT WITH NATURE, EVEN IF YOU SPEND MOST OF YOUR TIME INDOORS

Patients in hospitals with a view of nature heal faster than those without, people who work in offices with windows get sick less frequently, and a recent study of elderly people found that those who don't venture outside are more prone to depression.

Try to get into nature at least several times each week, and if you can't get outside use a screensaver of a beautiful natural scene or put a bunch of flowers or a plant on your desk.

4. SAY 'NO' MORE OFTEN

If you find yourself constantly putting other people's needs ahead of your own, practise saying 'no' more often. You may find it helps to have some phrases on hand that will buy you a bit of breathing space before you commit. Try, 'I'll need to get back to you on that,' for starters, and then create a few of your own.

5. QUIT

We live in a culture that tells us that winning (or, at the very least, finishing) is everything. In some cases, quitting or admitting you've made a wrong choice takes as much courage as hanging in there.

If you've tried everything to improve your work situation or an important relationship and your instinct tells you it really is time to let it go, maybe it's time to listen.

Accept imperfection

Perfectionism often stems from a desire to quell anxiety by controlling our external environments.

While some of these qualities might be useful, being a full-blown perfectionist can also be crippling. It can stop you from pursuing activities other than those you're good at, and it sometimes means that you procrastinate before completing difficult tasks. You may even give up too easily when something is extra difficult.

Perfectionists have a tendency to be overly cautious and sometimes unnecessarily thorough, causing a simple task to take hours. Maybe the most depleting aspect for the perfectionist is that within their own mind, there is very little room for error.

 Accept imperfection

How do you know if you're a perfectionist? Answer the following questions. They may indicate whether you have perfectionistic tendencies.

- Are you constantly trying to improve things?

- Do you agonise over the smallest details?

- Do you avoid trying new things for fear of making a mistake?

- Are you someone who imposes strict rules on yourself (constant dieting, rigid exercise campaigns or other 'rules' about how you should live)?

- Are you overly critical of yourself when you make a small mistake?

- Do you feel compelled to straighten pictures, reorganise filing systems or line up objects at home or work?

If you find yourself answering 'yes' to even one of the above, you may be inclined towards unhelpful habits.

GRADUALLY CHANGE YOUR WAYS

Cognitive behaviour psychologists recommend that the best approach to overcoming perfectionism is gradual exposure to change.

- Start by trying to catch yourself in the habit of trying to be perfect and see if you can let some things slide.

- If you're someone who is overly vigilant, try taking a less thorough approach.

- Attempt something new that you know you'll be less than perfect at.

Choose love

Of all the elements most likely to make us happy, at the top of the list is love. Regardless of how busy or stressed we become, we need to remember that our relationships matter most, even though they will challenge us from time to time.

On the more difficult days, remind yourself of the positive attributes of the other person and actively *choose* love.

- If you're struggling with a relationship but suspect it might be salvageable, make a commitment to work your way through your differences instead of giving up on it too soon.

- Get to know the different ways you demonstrate love for each other. Some people show love through affection or kind words, others through actions or deeds, others through giving gifts and others through making time for each other.

From time to time, put the other person's needs ahead of your own.

Learn to communicate openly. Volunteer information rather than making the people closest to you drag the words out of you.

DON'T EXPECT YOUR PARTNER, A FAMILY MEMBER OR FRIEND TO SINGLE-HANDEDLY MEET EVERY ONE OF YOUR NEEDS. INSTEAD, ACCEPT THAT THE DIFFERENT PEOPLE IN YOUR LIFE CAN COLLECTIVELY FILL YOU UP.

Laugh together.

Give up the need to be right all the time. Instead of constantly correcting your partner, let some things go through to the keeper.

(50) Choose love

- Discover at least one shared interest but, equally, respect that it's healthy to spend time apart (and even time alone).

- Prioritise spending time one-on-one (for couples, this is important even when you have young children).

- Every relationship is imperfect and many can even become difficult at times.

- Support each other. Be kind, loyal and respectful.

- Forgive often.

Extra reading & resources

BOOKS

Finding Your Own North Star by Martha Beck

The Gifts of Imperfection by Brené Brown

The Artist's Way by Julia Cameron

Tonglen, the Path of Transformation by Pema Chödrön

Grit by Angela Lee Duckworth

Man's Search for Meaning by Viktor Frankl

The Mindful Path to Self-Compassion by Christopher Germer

The Seven Principles for Making Marriage Work by John Gottman and Nan Silver

Constructive Wallowing by Tina Gilbertson

Extra reading & resources

The Happiness Trap by Russ Harris

Getting the Love You Want by Harville Hendrix

Believe in Yourself & Do What You Love by Kate James

Be Mindful & Simplify Your Life by Kate James

Feel the Fear and Do It Anyway by Susan Jeffers

If Not Dieting, Then What? by Rick Kausman

Your Life Matters by Petrea King

Drive by Daniel H Pink

Zig Zag by Keith Sawyer

Authentic Happiness by Martin Seligman

Learned Optimism by Martin Seligman

The Power of Now by Eckhart Tolle

IF YOU'RE SUFFERING FROM MENTAL ILLNESS

beyondblue.org.au

blackdoginstitute.org.au

If you're in Australia, speak to your GP about a mental health plan for access to financial support when you see a psychologist.

WEBSITES

VOLUNTEERING
goodcompany.com.au

POSITIVE NEWS
positive.news
goodnewsnetwork.org

DISCOVER YOUR PURPOSE PROGRAM
totalbalance.com.au/discover-your-purpose/

FREE GUIDED MEDITATIONS
totalbalance.com.au/positive-thinking-meditation/
totalbalance.com.au/body-scan-meditation/
insighttimer.com

REFERENCES

Chapter 4 – Challenge your baseline
nymag.com/scienceofus/2014/06/how-much-of-your-own-happiness-can-you-control.html

Chapter 6 – Deal with the Ds
questforlife.com.au/_literature_69327/Happiness_Is_an_Inside_Job

Chapter 8 – Cultivate compassion
nymag.com/scienceofus/2016/04/the-not-so-secret-secret-to-happiness-be-kinder-to-yourself-okay.html

Chapter 9 – Accept uncertainty
nature.com/ncomms/2016/160329/ncomms10996/full/ncomms10996.html

Chapter 16 – Make friends with money
Wellbeing: The Five Essential Elements by Tom Rath and Jim Harter

Chapter 23 – Write your way to a solution
theguardian.com/science/2009/feb/15/psychology-usa

Chapter 28 – Be more optimistic
health.harvard.edu/heart-health/optimism-and-your-health

Chapter 29 – Balance your optimism

livescience.com/2030-downside-optimism.html

psychologytoday.com/blog/think-well/201101/why-optimism-
can-be-bad-your-mental-health

ncbi.nlm.nih.gov/pmc/articles/PMC3807005/

Chapter 39 – Look for the good

psychologytoday.com/blog/anger-in-the-age-
entitlement/201212/one-thing-will-ruin-perfectly-good-
relationship

Chapter 42 – Embrace creativity

healthypsych.com/link-creativity-happiness/

psychologytoday.com/blog/arts-and-health/201109/art-and-
happiness

inc.com/christina-desmarais/25-ways-to-be-more-creative.
html

unc.edu/home/rksawyer/zigzag/the-model/ask.php

Chapter 44 – Relax your body

huffingtonpost.com.au/entry/stress-relief-that-
works_n_3842511

psychologytoday.com/blog/the-science-willpower/201105/
hugging-yourself-reduces-physical-pain

Chapter 46 – Practise gratitude

forbes.com/sites/amymorin/2014/11/23/7-scientifically-proven-benefits-of-gratitude-that-will-motivate-you-to-give-thanks-year-round/#51997af46800

Chapter 50 – Choose love

psychologytoday.com/blog/compassion-matters/201312/what-it-really-means-be-in-love

Also by
Kate James

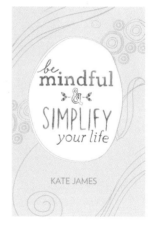

Available at totalbalance.com.au